FINANCIAL INTELLI(
SCHOOL BUSINES!

CW00589797

Husham has over 20 years' experience across five local authorities as a school business leader (SBL) and was in the first cohort to successfully complete the CSBM and DSBM programmes. Husham is a member of the Association of BAME Business Leaders in Education (ABBLed) advisory panel.

Husham's career path has ranged from Chief Financial Officer in Academy Trusts to Chief Executive Officer and Director of Learning of two school improvement companies. He currently works for drb Schools and Academies Services as a School Business Manager specialising in school financial management.

In 2003 Husham developed the financial training framework for all schools in Birmingham, which to this day still runs, and has trained thousands of SBMs, Head Teachers, Governors and Trustees. He also developed and led on the National Executive Leaders Programme in 2015 which brought together SBLs and Executive Head Teachers under one roof for the first time, training them simultaneously, and raising the status of the SBL profession within MATs.

Husham has been instrumental in raising the profile of SBLs including being the West Midlands SBM advocate for the National College for Teaching and Leadership (NCTL) in leading the regional strategy, and he was also part of the working parties which developed the SLE role and SFVS framework.

HUSHAM KHAN

FINANCIAL INTELLIGENCE FOR SCHOOL BUSINESS LEADERS

With special thanks to my family,

Sally Boaden and Clare Huxley

CONTENTS

Acknowledgements

I remember back in the Summer of 1995, sitting down-headed at my parents' kitchen table, telling my mother that I had not passed my second year at university and had a student debt as long as my arm. I remember that sinking feeling of having let someone down, big time, as well as myself. I literally wanted the whole ground to swallow me up. Life is full of these moments, which make us laugh and cry, but they also define us and make us who we are. It's what they call fight or flight. I recall asking my mother to make it all go away and to help me pay my student debt. She then said those words, which I did not fully understand until probably 15 years later but have stayed with me every single day since then. She said, "We can guide you but only you can sort this out."

That was the best advice I ever had and since that day I have never looked back but it changed my outlook on failure. Failure can affect any part of our lives, whether it is professionally or even our own mental health. We are human after all.

My second defining moment was when I was 24 years old; I had finally graduated from university, had applied for about 300 jobs and was not getting anywhere. My partner back then (now my wife), took me to a temping agency and there was a 3 month temping job at the finance department of a local council. This would be my first proper job in the business world, and walking into that job agency on that day has shaped my whole career and direction of travel going forwards. I am not sure where I would be now if I had not stepped through those doors and I most definitely would not be writing this book!

From my own experience, it has been more about direction rather than destination but it is those lessons from failure which shape our attitude and destiny.

Foreword

About Cheryl

I am a practising School Business Professional in a large secondary school in South East London. I have been in my role since September 2019 and absolutely love it, and love the school that I work in. Prior to taking up this role I was a school business manager in a primary school for two and a half years and before that in another primary school for just over one year (15 months to be exact). Having been in the profession for just under six years, I still feel like a newcomer to the party but in reality it's been an eventful time from almost the word go.

I joined the London Plus Association of SBMs, became Vice Chair, and helped to organise a regional conference. I contributed to The School Business Manager's Handbook published in 2018 by Hayley Dunn (what a thrill it was to see my name in print!) I then went on to win a professional development scholarship in 2019 from the US based Association of School Business Officials. I was one of 18 recipients of the Emerging Leaders Scholarship (and the only one from the UK). As part of the scholarship award I was given a free place at their national conference in Maryland, USA. The experience can only be described as amazing.

Giddy from the experience of my trip to America, I went into 2020 on a high. Despite the challenges of the worldwide coronavirus pandemic, I made the decision to form an association of my own – ABBLed. It was partly due to this that I found myself as one of the recipients of the CEO award for exceptional contribution to school business leadership from ISBL CEO Stephen Morales. Fast forward to 2021 and I was named as the TES School Business Leader of the Year. After achieving runner up status the previous year, this was a great honour. Goodness knows what the next five years will bring!

Meeting Husham

In 2020 I took the decision to form ABBLed (the Association of BAME Business Leaders in Education) with a view to tackling the low levels of ethnic diversity in the profession. I knew it would be a huge task and so I put feelers out for SBL colleagues to come onboard to form an advisory panel. Husham Khan contacted me to volunteer his services. I did a bit of digging and was told that he was "a big deal with loads of knowledge and experience". With this ringing endorsement I snapped his hand off and welcomed him aboard. From June 2020 he officially became an advisor to the ABBLed board.

During the pandemic, ABBLed meetings were all online so I was able to "meet" Husham very quickly. My first impression of him was that he was very quiet but as time went on I soon realised that those quiet moments were usually a sign of Husham scribbling away in his notes until his opportunity arose to share with the rest of the team. Almost every time he shares a thought with the group it results in a "penny drop" moment for the rest of us. Husham has a unique way of quietly delivering ideas that change your whole viewpoint on the task at hand; and it's always for the better.

The book

There are several books available that are aimed at helping SBPs to get a better understanding of how school finance works. However, there is nothing quite like "Financial Intelligence for School Business Leaders". Husham takes the topic of school finance and approaches it through a different lens that seeks to equip the readers with the tools to interpret their trust or school's financial position. Readers are taken step by step through a number of metrics and KPIs and are guided through, not only how to use them, but why they are important (obviously, my favourite is the ABBLed ratio!)

Husham developed the financial training framework for all schools across Birmingham and has trained thousands of SBMs as well as Head Teachers and Governors. Husham's wealth of experience spans over 20 years and I can't think of anyone better placed to advise and guide School Business Leaders on how to develop their financial intelligence. He really is an expert in this area.

Husham has long demonstrated a passion for using financial information in a meaningful way. In writing this book he invites readers into his world and takes them on a journey to understanding how and why financial intelligence plays an integral part in school planning. After reading this book SBPs will be able to build up a catalogue of meaningful metrics to use in reporting but also to feed into long term planning.

This is a book for School Business Professionals at all levels who can take the information and transform their use of financial information. It's an invaluable tool for Head Teachers, the rest of the leadership team and Governors, and quite frankly it will be a constant on the #SBMReadingList.

Introduction

'Leaders will always create their own pathway.'

Husham Khan

I started to write this book back in April 2020 and I quickly realised that despite my 20 years plus experience in school business leadership, there were many unexplored concepts and areas within the field of financial intelligence in schools. As we continue to transition out of the global pandemic and into a world where renewed efficiency, zoom meetings and risk management become the norm, I wanted to explore how schools can best analyse their financial information in a more effective and useful way.

Throughout this journey, I have encountered many strategies and formulas which schools use to both analyse and present their data. With no, one definitive point of call available, I decided to unpick what I knew was being used in the field and combine it with new ways of thinking, original business concepts, and ideas from other sectors such as sport and commerce.

This book begins by asking you to rethink how you see your financial data and how this aligns with the main drivers in your school or trust. It then dives deep into the many areas of financial awareness and analysis, which drive core decision making in the education sector.

By rethinking how you see your school's budget, this book will provide the reassurance and knowledge to support better decision making within your setting.

I hope you enjoy reading this book as much as I have enjoyed writing it, and I hope you get as much from reading it as I did from researching and writing it.

Chapter 1

Retraining Your Brain

'The progression of how we apply our knowledge is the natural evolution of any profession.' *Khan 2021*

Changing the way we see things

In education, the role of school business leader means so many things to so many people. Over the last 20 years we have seen probably the most rapid development of the profession, with so many pathways and specialisms available to branch off into.

With models of schools being so varied and unique to academy trusts, groups of schools and individual schools, it was only a matter of time when the way we view financial data would need to change.

Through financial intelligence, the way we use financial data is evolving and it is still the case, in most schools, that there is limited understanding in this area from governors and trustees to school business leaders, including head teachers, school business managers and chief financial officers. The main mechanisms of financial compliance, whether it is local authority returns for maintained schools or academy returns to the ESFA, do not focus heavily enough on financial metrics other than through their limited respective resource toolkits. This has caused a knowledge gap in the types of metrics schools have available to use, but more importantly it has created a gap in the metrics schools should be using.

From my own experience, the way financial metric data is used is not totally understood but it has the potential to become far more powerful if it is fully understood and recognised for the benefits it can bring to trust boards and governing bodies.

This book will be focusing on the data analysis side of school financial management, what it means and how this can be best put into practice to influence decision making. With risk and internal scrutiny becoming more staple requirements for all forms of internal school audit and directives of the Academy Trust Handbook, the way we look at financial data is changing as we constantly seek better ways of analysing financial reports and other useful data.

Public sector values versus private sector practices

The very mention of the words 'private sector' or 'business' within state education would have raised eyebrows a few years ago. Now I see it as a necessity and, dare I say, a requirement. You might go as far as to say, it should even be 'private sector values versus public sector practices'. The last decade has seen just over half of the pupil population being taught in academies; this has introduced a more business-led approach to school business management, and the way we manage and report public money. As schools look to constantly seek out the optimum model for teaching, learning and support services, it is difficult to argue against having private sector values in the state education sector. I know many executive head teachers whose approach to running their trusts has shifted over the last five years from public sector values to private sector values. This shift in mind-set cannot be underestimated and a more reasonable approach would be to pivot based on the situation or circumstances being presented. For example, the management of staff within a team may require more of a focus on public sector values. The decision making on a budget, in particular, if you are looking to prioritise costs may require more of a focus on private sector values.

The mind block (or unblock!)

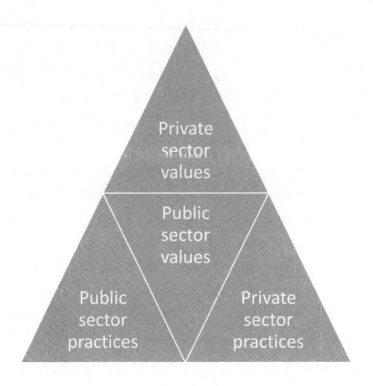

Khan, 2021

Schools will use a multitude of drivers to run their organisations and I often see a tug of war between balancing public sector and private sector values. As schools have become more commercially aware through a financial lens, their financial practices have also become more corporate and rigorous. This is something which needed to happen and we have seen these strengthened from year to year through DfE / LA directives and the Academy Trust Handbook. Maybe there is a place for a mixture of the above values and practices but it is the private ones which are increasingly becoming more dominant in the sector. The values and practices may also vary depending on whether governance, business or pedagogy are being explored.

This is an exercise I would recommend any senior leadership team or trust board to carry out. As a compass, it can steer school improvement but is far more useful as a challenge tool to turn preconceptions team members may have upside down, providing a constructive and critical approach to leadership. Comfort zones can be dangerous and this is there to tempt team members out of the norm and in to a creative space.

The pyramid becomes more useful when it is applied to financial management and ICFP (integrated curriculum financial planning). The pyramid is not a one-size-fits-all approach and the segments may be shifted around. The most important segments are the top area and the middle area. From the above diagram you could conclude that the school's business strategy has a corporate spearhead but much of the central decision making has its traits and drivers taken from public sector values and this is at the heart of the diagram.

Return on investment

Education and return on investment very rarely get mentioned in the same sentence. The very idea of pupils as commodities goes against the fundamentals of teaching and the ethics of the education world. About 10 years ago, I introduced this to governors and it was met with a lot of resistance and questioning as to whether this language had a place in education. I completely understood their stance on this and, as a parent, I would struggle to understand and accept this as well.

Fast forward five years and return on investment is being used far more widely, and certainly over the last three years, there has been a lot more acceptance of this practice and the way it is used. The way we view finance in schools has changed and it is important that we also view finance as an indicator of how effective income and expenditure is or needs to be.

Return on investment, in its rawest form, means how do you get the biggest bang for your buck? How do pupils achieve the best outcomes for the financial investment made in them? The only measure we have for this is expenditure versus results. The results would be in the form of attainment outcomes and progress. This can be misleading, especially in areas of high free school meals. How do you measure pupil welfare, health and mental outcomes? We can measure attendance but for a more holistic measure of return on investment, as many things as possible should be used to arrive at the measure of return on investment.

Finance versus educational outcomes

The evidence of any link between spending in schools and educational attainment is very limited. This may be because there is not a one-size-fits-all approach to provision in schools, the historical funding variances across the country and the different models of schools across the system.

The research studies which do exist on English data provide a limited estimate of the impact of school spending on educational attainment. The evidence does show that the greater the amount of resources a school has at its disposal, the greater the upwards influence on educational attainment. Due to the limited information in this area, this research is only available at primary level. The same research also shows that additional spending has a positive impact on the attainment of disadvantaged pupils.

The Sutton Trust has carried out extensive research in to the most effective strategies used for pupil premium funding. In Ofsted's publication on 'Making the Cut' and the Sutton Trust research on effective pupil premium strategies, it is more likely that the way money is spent, the greater the positive influence this has on educational attainment.

For many years, the rate of increase in school funding for most schools has not kept pace with rising costs. The last 2 years has seen this intensify to such a degree that the government introduced the teachers' pay grant and the teachers' pension grant, which has been assumed within a school's main funding from 2021. There has also been a positive impact on Ofsted outcomes, even with several significant revisions to the framework. The proportion of schools over the last 10 years that are judged good or outstanding has increased.

Three, six, twelve makes one

For the purpose of this section I will mainly be referring to the external reports normally presented to governors and trustees at finance committees.

The regularity of financial reporting became more frequent about two years ago when the Academy Trust Handbook recommended the strengthening in the maintaining of financial oversight of funds.

When the gradual delegation of funding to schools took place in the 1990s, the financial reporting requirements to finance committees were, at their best, termly and three times per year. If we fast forward 25 years, not much has changed in this regularity, but we have seen more regularity in internal reporting, namely the academies sector through monthly management accounts. The maintained sector does not have such an emphasis on regularity of internal financial reporting, but it should still take place. One of the main financial stress factors during the Coronavirus pandemic has been shocks to private income and supply budgets. The only way to accurately track these large and irregular movements in income and expenditure is to carry out regular and monthly internal reporting as well as three to five year financial forecasting simultaneously. This is a step change in the way we present projections as its frequency will move from termly to monthly regularity.

The advantage of this is more accurate, real time financial intelligence for senior leaders to support improved financial planning with constant alignment to the priorities within the school's development plan.

By using more regular, long term forecasting, the amount of data available for metric analysis will be hugely increased. This will allow senior leaders and finance committees to challenge the financial data on a more intricate level through dissection of the data. This does promote financial analysis of the school's data in more of forensic accounting style, but this is the additional layer of analysis needed to support better decision making at a time when income has not kept up with increases in expenditure.

Top tips - Critical grid

When was the last time the governors or trust board evaluated the school's vision along with the school's business strategy. The following can be used by governors or the trust board to check, align, or set if necessary, the overall vision for the school. It takes in to account the thinking around Khan's Mind Block and what areas can be challenged to inform vision and affect the school's strategy and direction.

Educational vision	Business vision
When was the last time you reviewed your school's vision?	Do you have a business vision?
Does your school's educational vision and business vision align?	
Does each school within the trust have its own vision or is there an overall trust vision (or both)?	How does this impact on the business of individual schools?
Is it time to realign your school / trust vision?	
How do the values and practices within Khan's Mind Block impact the school's vision and strategy?	

Chapter 2

The What, How and Why of Metrics and KPIs

Challenge the Norm!

Quite often we see different KPIs and metrics within education without fully understanding their use, meaning or outcomes. For many years, schools have used benchmarking and it has served more of a tick box for annual compliance with national standards, rather than being properly utilised to guide the strategy and direction of school improvement and financial discipline.

Why we use metrics and KPIs must be fully understood by school leaders, in particular governors and trustees, otherwise it is an opportunity missed and provides less measurement and accountability on an organisation's strategy.

Metrics and KPIs have been used for decades in companies in their constant pursuit of efficiency, growth and understanding key indicators to financial performance and consumer habits.

In schools, the consumer is the pupil, as well as the legal guardian, and we should not shy away from thinking in this way. It is definitely worth seeing how Khan's Mind Block' works in your school so that you can assess the business culture.

Metrics are not KPIs

One of the things which is most misunderstood in school financial management is when, how and why we use metrics and KPIs. In order to decide this we must first understand the distinction between the two. I have seen several definitions of these areas on their own but very little to describe them when they are both being used.

Metrics are a type of measure which are used to evaluate and monitor the various aspects of a business. It can be argued that because there is more financial data available, metrics are broader than KPIs.

KPIs are a subdivision of metrics and allow the measurement of specific areas of a business. Trend analysis and KPIs are normally carried out and analysed together as how we search for business improvements to ultimately raise performance.

When was the last time you really spent time on looking at which KPIs and metrics are important to your school?

The Why

We use KPIs and metrics in schools so that we can align the staff, school policy, processes and systems with the objectives of the school, including the school improvement plan. There are many benefits that this type of detailed analysis can bring.

- They may bring to light areas of the budget, including financial inefficiencies and underperformance. This may extend to efficiency in the deployment of staff.
- Allow analysis at a segmental level of individual departments, budget holders, or even individual staff. It's a great way to monitor accountability.
- We all know how important cash flow is, and this area cannot be underestimated. Cash flow over the longer term is becoming more and more important in an era of funding increasing at a lower rate than overall inflationary increases (note, not necessarily overall spending as these are different things).
- It is important that KPIs allow there to be not only measureable targets, but goals to achieve, so that expenditure fits within a defined budget envelope. Without targets, there is little point in using KPIs and metrics to measure.
- Definitely an area which is under used is sharing the overall budget position and KPIs with staff. It is important for staff to buy in to why KPIs are used and how this directly impacts on their day to day decision making. We are all in this together.
- The use of RAG rating in KPIs has been used for many years but it is still fairly new within education. It is a great tool, especially when used by non-finance professionals.

Misconceptions with KPIs and things to avoid

Just because a KPI appears on a predefined chart does not mean you have to use it. I often see KPIs listed which do not mean an awful lot, when it would be far more meaningful to swap them for more useful KPIs. There are several issues to be aware of when developing and using KPIs:

- It is important to use KPIs in the correct way. If KPIs are not used in the correct way, the feedback and information received may not be as useful. If senior leaders use KPIs as a stick to encourage the better performance of staff, staff may find a way to work around any targets which have been set and the feedback and information which was originally intended to be used may not be accurate or useful at all.
- Any KPIs which are set and communicated must accurately reflect the intentions of the school and what is trying to be achieved. If this is not communicated properly, staff may follow the KPIs too rigidly, at a possible loss in quality and the strategy of the school's business may be completely missed or even forgotten in the process.
- Financial KPIs tend to only mention the goal of what needs to be achieved rather than how the strategy should be communicated to staff. How an outcome can be achieved and a KPI is vital to the outcome of a financial target. They go hand in hand. In this case, it again comes down to the communication of the strategy.

- When looking at any type of KPI across a school, the financial KPIs may be the most reliable ones as they are based on actual financial data. This could be seen as an over reliance on historic data rather than forward looking as they reflect on performance in the past and do not always predict the future due to variables and uncertainty. Due to this, some financial KPIs may not be useful for future business performance and may not form part of the school's overall strategy.
- The greatest misconception of KPIs is that they are regularly confused with real performance, especially where there is a bonus incentive. All a KPI does is to give an indicator of performance. How employees interpret a KPI may influence their behaviour to a degree where it is only taken at face value. This could be counterproductive to the aim of the KPI and may do more harm than good.

Choosing the right metrics and KPIs

One of the things I see regularly at board and finance committee level in schools is a long list of KPIs being presented as part of a tick box compliance exercise without a full understanding of the data available. If you have the data, you might as well make use of it!

By making a few small adjustments in the way we look at this data, it is possible to turn a list of KPIs into a powerful business-focused tool linked directly to the school's overall improvement strategy.

The high level metrics such as income, expenditure, cash flow and reserves, as well as staffing, will be key and this should be the starting point. The choice of using the correct KPIs will be important to help your business structure improve its processes.

By selecting the correct KPIs you are not only saving time in focusing on what is going to make a difference but they will support in monitoring efficiency and help the different departments keep aligned with the overall business metrics of the school.

Employees are key

By far the most important area of a school's budget is the staffing. This is where KPI analysis really comes in to its own and with better tools and awareness recently, schools have been able to forensically drill down in to their staffing structures to better see how finance and curriculum are interlinked.

Develop your own KPIs

The following table was adapted from Neely et al. (1996) and is still as relevant today. It provides a useful framework to help you create KPIs for your own school.

Top tips - Performance measurement sheet

Title	What is the KPI?
Purpose	What is the reason for measurement of performance?
Relates to	What high level objective of the business do you want to measure? This is important because any feedback will be used to inform change and bring improvements within the business.
Target	What needs to be achieved and by when?
Formula	How is the KPI calculated? The KPI may have a direct impact on behaviour.
Frequency	How often will this KPI be measured and reviewed?
Who measures	Which staff member in responsible for this?
Source of data	Where is the data source being taken from and over which period?
Who is accountable	Who is responsible for taking action on the KPI?
What they do	What action people should take to improve the performance of this KPI.

Chapter 3

The Bottom Line

Is cash really king?

This is an area governors find one of the most challenging as there are still schools which do not do enough to fully explain the relationship between cash in their bank account, cash flow and reserves.

In an economic environment where money is tight, it is essential for schools who manage their finances through a bank account, to not only maintain a positive cash flow, but plan for a positive cash flow, taking into account any potential future drops in income such as pupil numbers or extra-curricular activities including lettings.

The cash position and cash flow of any school should be treated with equal importance to the estimated end-of-year position and the future financial projections of a school. This is because the estimated end-of-year position and cash balance (as a result of careful cash flow planning) are directly related with common trends among difference phases of school.

Cash balance versus reserves

Throughout the sector there are differing level of reserves when compared to cash balances in the bank. The difference between phases of schools is wide and depending on the phase type, has been either increasing or decreasing over the last 5 years.

One measure we should actively be using, as well as comparing the figures to historical and sector average data, is the ratio of cash in bank to the free reserves. For the purpose of this comparison free reserves are classed as the total of unrestricted reserves and restricted general reserves.

For example, we have seen the ratio comparing cash and reserves in the primary sector moving downwards by 14% over 5 years as the sector has been impacted by funding geared more towards the secondary sector. This has led to an average cash to reserves ratio of 1.2:1, having reduced from 1.5:1, a decrease of 20% on the ratio. In cash terms this would mean cash in the bank being £600,000 and reserves being £500,000, hence the 1.2:1 ratio.

The secondary sector has moved the other way over the last 5 years with a 7% increase in the average cash to reserves ratio of 1.5:1. Part of this could be attributed to the increase in the national AWPU minimum funding weighting which was applied to secondary school funding.

Multi academy trusts (MATs) have seen little movement on the average cash to reserves ratio over the last 5 years. This could be down to the rapid expansion of chains and the increase of centralisation with MATs. Expansion of trusts may incur an initial outlay which exceeds any additional expansion funding and it can take several years for true economies of scale to come to fruition. I would like to see more data on the cash to reserves ratio comparing different sizes of trusts with each other. This would be useful benchmarking data to highlight best practice and structures of MATs.

NFF / GAG income ratios

The Coronavirus pandemic has placed more emphasis on how schools look at income and especially areas of the budget which are trading entities. Examples of these are music tuition, before and after schools clubs, and sports lettings.

In order to examine a school's core funding versus overall income we must first establish what funding streams we are comparing.

NFF (national funding formula) funding and GAG income are effectively the same thing and is the funding a school receives based on the NFF which uses the same universal principles to work out the level for which a school is funded.

For those of you who are new to the academies sector, GAG stands for general annual grant and is the term used for core funding of academies. For the purposes of this area, NFF funding will be used to describe the core funding for maintained schools, although it is also commonly referred to as section 251 funding. The latter narrative is technically untrue as section 251 funding is far wider.

The GAG income ratio is not commonly used within the education sector but recent events have brought this little known KPI to the foreground. Its importance during and post-recession cannot be underestimated as it is a useful indicator to measure a school's reliance on core GAG funding compared to other funding a school may receive. For the purpose of this comparison, other funding could be pupil premium, exceptional SEN funding and private income to name but a few.

Example of GAG Income ratio

GAG income <u>divided by</u> Overall income

(Please note that this excludes any B/Fwd balances).

This will give you a percentage figure. The higher the percentage figure the more reliant the school is on its core GAG funding and the less reliant it is on external income. There are two ways you can interpret this data. The first is the school may receive very little additional funding, especially anything where deprivation funding is low due to the socioeconomic make-up of the local population. Any calculations using this formula should be pre any top slice or pooling, for example central MAT or Federation charges.

The following table shows some possible reasons and risks behind high and low GAG income ratios:

Reason / Risk	High GAG Income ratio	Low GAG Income ratio
Reasons	Low area of deprivation affecting additional funding e.g. pupil premium.	High area of deprivation affecting additional funding.
	Low additional opportunities of private income generation.	High additional private income.
	High area of deprivation and lower skilled community (affecting additional private income).	More densely populated area.
	Rural location / community.	Urban / city setting.
Risks	Over reliance on government funding.	Higher risk to income in a recession.
	Under-utilisation of facilities and loss of pupils to other establishments.	Higher risk to income in a pandemic.

From a MAT perspective this type of exercise is very important as it can show the range of different commercial opportunities individual schools have in place. It is certainly not a one-size-fits-all approach when it comes to additional income generation, but there may be positive practices, which can be seized upon and expanded within individual or groups of schools.

The benchmarks for GAG income ratios differ significantly between primary, secondary and MATs. Within the primary sector the average ratio is around 73% but when we look at the secondary sector it increases to 78%. A factor in the difference between the phases is the amount of additional income which can be generated when compared to the overall income a school brings in each year through funding, grants and other income. Secondary schools mainly have more pupils and may not charge for some extra-curricular clubs. They also do not receive UIFSM (universal free school meals). Both these factors could have an impact on the ratio which could increase the ratio due to less additional income. MATs tend to be mainly primary in membership and the average ratio is 73% which is to be expected.

Grant income ratio (ABBLed ratio)

A new ratio which was developed by Khan during the pandemic and was first used by ABBLed (Association of BAME business leaders in education) is the ABBLed ratio. The unique nature of this ratio is that it looks at all grant funding the school has, for example, GAG, pupil premium etc. and then divides this by the overall grant income plus other income or private income.

Private income is defined as income from parents and other sources of self-generated income outside of government funding.

Example of ABBLed ratio

Grant funding <u>divided by</u> (Grant funding plus private income)

This will give you a percentage figure. The higher the percentage figure the more reliant the school is on its core grant funding (GAG, PP, PE & sport premium) and the less reliant it is on external income. This can be a good thing and a bad thing as less private income means less financial exposure to a pandemic because the budget was already set low for private income. It does mean that there may be less commercial activity for the school due to less private income coming in.
On the other hand, if you have high commercial activity planned, you have more private income coming in but you are more at risk in a pandemic and your ratio will be lower. As a measure and benchmark if you are looking to mitigate against the risk of a pandemic it is better to have a higher ABBLed ratio, hence less private income planned. It works really well within MATs as you can compare the risk or exposure of each school. I would advise adding this to the schools strategic risk register as it is a really useful KPI to use which is easy for governors to use.

Any calculations using this formula should be pre any top slice or pooling, for example central MAT or Federation charges.

Example of ABBLEd ratio MAT comparator

The following chart shows an example of the ABBLed ratio across a MAT. Each of the nine schools has their own ratio and there is an average for the trust. This level of analysis provides a quick strategic overview of schools which are more susceptible to a loss of income during a significant event such as a pandemic. It is also a valuable tool to examine which schools are making the most of commercial opportunities and which schools could improve their commercial activity.

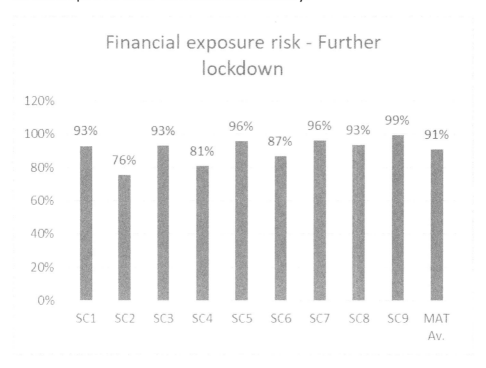

In-year position (operational margin)

This is an area of metrics which surprisingly still gets overlooked, especially where cumulative end of year surpluses have been high over a number of years. The main reason for this would be the level of understanding among governors and the lack of training available for governors.

The in-year position (also known as structural position) of any particular year, within a school's accounts or budget projections, is often the precursor to analysing other areas of the budget, especially KPIs. I regularly see in-year positions driving KPIs in other areas, when it would be far better for KPIs to drive the in-year position. This is a little known concept used and created by Khan known as 'Constant KPIs'.

'Constant KPIs are the regular use of KPIs to achieve a specific objective which is monitored with regular frequency. Also known as Khan's 'Constant,' *Khan, 2021*

In order to understand how an in-year impact has occurred, all areas of the school's budget need to be examined. It could be a combination of several factors or just one. We often see a drop in pupil numbers and one off expenditures (exceptional items), triggering in-year deficits. The pandemic saw a chasm of in-year financial impacts between different phases of schools, with stark differences between 5 - 18 and early year's settings. Much of the increase in in-year deficits within early years was due to the significant negative impact on private income, although furlough did soften the blow slightly.

Particular staffing issues, such as long term sickness, one off capital expenditure and even a poor judgement by Ofsted, can trigger anomalies in spending to such a degree that the in-year deficit does not show the true picture. This is why constant KPIs are important so that it is not just a once every 12 month exercise, but a tool to constantly evaluate the strategic financial objectives of the school, preferably in line with financial reporting cycles of six times per year.

An in-year deficit cannot be seen in isolation and it is often the case that further drilling down in to the budget will be required.

Back to the future!

Sustainability should be at the centre of every school budget, but it is the long term future predictions which should be treated with equal importance to a current financial year. The whole reason for long term financial planning is to allow time for a school to make the changes it needs, whether it is to a staffing structure or non-staffing areas. In order to understand where a school's financial positon will be in three to five years' time, it is vital that the historic budget picture is understood, as this likely to drive decision making in the present to influence the future.

I would recommend new Head Teachers and SBLs in a school to carry out a full review of their budget but to also look at the previous two years to support in building the history of the current financial position.

Another tip for new leaders in a school, with responsibility for financial management, is to actually go back and apply KPI analysis to previous years. We will come on to this later on and what KPIs are most useful for different situations. This is useful for schools which have a large in year or cumulative deficit and in depth KPI analysis can be effective in controlling and reducing the deficit.

Pupil numbers

With pupil numbers predicted to be lower overall in the education system due to birth rates, Brexit and the pandemic, the marketing of schools and competition for pupils has never been fiercer.

This is also one of the most under-rated areas of a budget but it is one of the easiest to plan for once you know the estimated pupil numbers you will be using. One of the common problems with this is lagged funding and I often see schools using data which is 12 months old to work out current KPIs. As a rule of thumb, if you are measuring per pupil financial metrics, such as spend, then it should be based on the number of pupils you have on roll at that particular time. For example, we will use an academy due to the extended lagged impact on funding when comparing pupil numbers which drive the GAG. Both the maintained and academy sector operate on a lagged funding basis but the academy sector has a lag of 11 months. This is because the pupil number census is completed in October, but this will drive funding which will not kick in until the following September.

Once you know your current pupil numbers and projected pupil numbers, as well as your financial information for the corresponding years, it should be easier to start comparing years and working out more detailed metrics for areas such as spend and income per pupil.

We do not see enough use of strategic data when planning future years' budgets for pupil numbers. The most accessible lists for pupil numbers up to 5 years in the future for primary and secondary admissions will be the ward data that local authorities produce, which show the impact on birth rates in different areas of a city, county or borough. Often these reports are followed by recommendations for increases and decreases in PAN size (published admission number) for different geographical locations, with decreases in PAN size often being decided based on Ofsted judgements.

Senior Leaders have access to other information which is available but is rarely used to estimate pupil numbers. Another useful list is the lists given to primary and secondary schools showing the number of times parents have included a school on the admission choice forms. The figures from these forms do not directly correlate to the September intake but they will be useful for planning if compared to the previous years' data and September intake. I would recommend looking back over 3 years if it is the first time this exercise is being undertaken. There will be trends which will show patterns that will help in planning future funding and intakes.

For schools where there is competition for places, often in city settings where population areas are dense, a top tip is to mark your intake on a map. If done over several years, you will be able see the boundary shape of the intake on a visual map. This is important as it shows cut off locations and it is a great visual challenge tool for SBLs to use in SLT to show how marketing in certain geographical areas can work by targeting specific mediums of communication to aid promotion of the school, and attract any potential new pupils and parents.

Cumulative position

The amount of money a school has left at the end of a financial year only tells part of the picture of showing how financially solvent a school is. If not properly understood it can hide a multitude of other issues which could manifest to provide severe financial challenges in years to come.

Any end of year position should always be taken in the context of several others factors. The in-year position of a school is probably the most important measure to precede the end-of-year position, followed by the percentage of the balance remaining on the predicted end-of-year position. Due to the strain on local authority finances, we have seen the control of surplus balance mechanism deployed more regularly to enable a distribution of surplus funds to other schools who may be struggling with their deficits. There are pros and cons where this is used with the most controversial being centred around how ethical it is to allow schools to build excessive reserves. The academies sector has lesser restrictions in this area but they have the added requirement for a reserves policy which normally takes into account the level of permitted reserves which are allowable and set at Trust level.

As a rule of thumb I commonly hear four weeks of funding would be a benchmark of what to aim to carry forward each year and slightly lower in the secondary sector. The cumulative position is linked very heavily to the cash flow position of a school and the two should be seen together to provide a more complete overview of how financially secure a school is. On this basis you could argue that one month of payroll cost for the entire staff could also be seen as another indicator of how much should remain in reserves. It is vital that where there are excessive reserves, the future commitment of those funds, conforms to the policy and timeline of how the funds should be utilised.

The cumulative positions on long term future predictions can provide cause for concern and forecasts, quite often, turn out to show large predictive deficits. This is where historic analysis of balances along with combining historic and predictive KPI analysis can become a strong tool to deploy as it will show the progressive financial journey the school has been on and will be embarking on.

This is a new term known as 'Progressive public sector finance' which Khan developed several years ago and uses in schools.

'Progressive public sector finance is combining historic and future financial metrics and KPIs to support the decision making process to change the financial direction of a school.' *Khan, 2021*

Exceptional spend or item

There are several reasons why a school may incur exceptional expenditure, but it is important to first understand what constitutes an exceptional item, followed by how we treat the item when it comes to financial reporting and more importantly, understanding how an item may impact on reporting.

The following items are considered to be exceptional items:

- Capital project.
- Redundancy and severance cost.
- Grant income or expenditure, especially if different financial years are impacted.
- Additional fixed term staff to raise standards in a specific area such as addressing outcomes from an Ofsted inspection or an area of progress linked to subject.
- A loss in income.
- Costs arising from damage or theft.
- Extra supply staff resulting in significant additional spend due to sickness or vacancies.
- Counterparty grant funding.

When analysing a financial report, there may be items which distort certain benchmarking, metrics or KPIs and it is important that any particular context or event is looked at together with the financial report and KPIs.

An example may be if there has been a grant for a particular project received in one year but not paid out of the schools budget until the following year. This would impact on areas such as the end of year position and KPIs such as staffing versus income.

During the pandemic there was a marked increase in exceptional items being reported at committee and board level such as cleaning cost, free school meals (FSM) and staffing.

Financial reports do not always tell the full story and the more narrative you have to explain anomalies, the greater the financial intelligence will be which will in turn lead to improved and more holistic decision making.

'Holistic decision making is using both tangible and intangible emotional intelligence to arrive at an informed decision.' *Khan, 2021*

Trading accounts

Commercialisation within schools used to be a dirty word but many schools use their premises, facilities and brand to generate additional revenues. As the improvement of curriculum development and training has shifted away from local authorities to a system-led approach over time, the opportunities for schools to own this space have expanded. The different models of teaching schools / hubs, research schools and CPD, have created self-sustaining trading entities within school budgets.

These opportunities bring greater reporting requirements when it comes to the bottom line. Where there are separately reportable grants and trading accounts, it is important to ensure that when looking at any end-of-year cumulative position, there is an understanding between the school's overall carry forward position and any other balances included within the carry forward which may need to be budgeted to be spent the following year. An example of this would be a specific grant a school receives to undertake a specific externally accountable and reportable initiative or project which is monitored within the schools accounts but is not a direct part of the school's normal activities. If there is any underspend in this particular initiative, it should be accounted for separately so that transparency of year-end balances can be demonstrated, including allocating any underspend to be spent in the following financial year. Capital funding should also be treated in a similar way so that it is separated from the main accounts, is identifiable (so that it can be reported), and does not distort or artificially inflate the over financial picture. Ideally, trading accounts within a school's main budget should have their own section where it is easy to view the income and expenditure. The school's monitoring report should be able to demonstrate the split in any estimated end-of-year position by separating the relevant main school budget, additional trading entities funded through grants (and separately reportable to a government agency) and capital.

Current ratio (liquidity ratio)

This is one of my favourite 'at-a-glance ratios' which tells us a lot from a couple of simple figures. The figures have become more prominent as the number of academies has increased and is often used during a due diligence review of a school's financial reports prior to becoming part of a MAT. This figure is used more for internal reporting rather than external but nonetheless, it has a place and should be used by SBLs as a measure of a school's financial health. For this reason, it is an important measure to have in place and to compare from year to year.

The current ratio measures a company's ability to pay current, or short-term, liabilities (debt and payables) with its current, or short-term, assets (cash, inventory, and receivables).

The current assets on a school's balance sheet represent the value of all assets that can reasonably be converted into cash within a 12 month period.

The current liabilities are the company's debts or obligations on its balance sheet that are due within a 12 month period.

The formula for calculating the current ratio is:

Current Ratio = Current Assets / Current Liabilities

For a worked example we are going to use a school which has current assets of £1.4m and current liabilities of £900,000.

Current Ratio = 1,400,000/900,000 = 1.56

In this case the current ratio is just above 1.5, which would be seen as an acceptable level to operate within. If the school had a current ratio of less than one, this may give cause for concern and be an indicator of poor financial health.

When considering the current ratio there may be fluctuations throughout the year, especially in schools which sell a lot of inventory, such as uniform. This could end up having an impact on the current ratio, therefore, it is important that the calculation is done at different times of the year to iron out any peaks and troughs. Like with any other metric or KPI, the current ratio should be analysed in conjunction with the context of the school and other measures to give a broader understanding of the school's overall financial performance.

Tops tips – Consider your measures

When was the last time you evaluated the internal financial reporting measures in your school. Successful businesses use a range of financial data especially when measuring sales performance. It should be no different in schools.

As a group, to include SLT and governors, assess the existing measures of financial performance the school uses including its frequency. How do these measures fit in with the school's overall vision, educational and business strategy and are they fit for purpose? Does the schools need to introduce new measures to improve its financial performance?

Use holistic decision making to make better decisions on the budget. By using hard financial data in conjunction with an understanding of what is happening on the ground in a school, from curriculum to staff wellbeing, resources can be allocated appropriately guided by informed emotional intelligence.

Chapter 4

What is Integrated Curriculum Financial Planning

Demystifying a myth

I often see schools approaching their budget planning, monitoring and reporting from a financial perspective only. I cannot blame them as much of the SBL training since 2002 has been focused mostly on the operational side of school business management and the roles SBLs have differs considerably with only some SBLs having a deep understanding of how a schools' curriculum works. The larger the school, the more important it is for SBLs to understand the relationship between the curriculum and finance.

Throughout this chapter we will be exploring the foundations of ICFP (Integrated curriculum financial planning), how to carry out your own review and the best ways to use the information produced from carrying out such an exercise.

Putting the curriculum first

ICFP takes an alternative approach to planning a budget by looking at what the curriculum requires to structurally resource it (how many teaching staff and support staff are required and how are they deployed) so that the following areas are covered and hopefully met:

- Meeting the needs of the pupils.
- A staffing structure which is efficient and flexible.

- Has raising standards at the heart of it.
- Achieves reasonable class sizes or option groups across the whole school and meets the challenges of individual year groups.
- Uses the curriculum to drive the budget.
- Maximises efficiencies and minimises inefficiencies through the management of staffing resources.
- Identifies key issues which may affect the effective use of resources.
- An affordable curriculum which is fit for purpose and is sustainable.
- Takes into account the requirements of Ofsted.
- Will achieve the best overall outcomes for pupils.
- Achieves a balance in how resources are deployed to optimise their impact on standards.

'ICFP is a curriculum led financial planning practice which helps achieve a balance in how resources are used to optimise the impact on teaching, learning and wellbeing.' *Khan, 2021*

Where to start

Before we look at the output of an ICFP review, it is important to understand where to begin with reviewing a school's ICFP. For the purposes of this exercise I have assumed there is little knowledge of the practices involved within the school and the person responsible for carrying out this exercise. The first time you carry out this exercise in a school is quite important, especially if you are carrying out a review of the existing deployment of staff. This will be at odds with ICFP as you are not creating a curriculum to plan financially, but you will be reviewing the finances of how a curriculum is delivered. They are two totally different concepts. One is curriculum-led and the other is finance-led. We will explore the difference between the two later on.

The starting point will be to make a list of everybody, both teaching and support staff, who are involved in delivering the curriculum. At this point, it must be stressed that this should include all members of SLT who are teachers and any HLTAs (higher level teaching assistant) who have contact time with a class. The latter is more prevalent in secondary schools but we are seeing it more and more within the primary sector due to lower costs.

Once you have a full list of the staff to use, include other information such as:

- FTE (full time equivalent number).
- The total cost of each staff member for the financial year. Remember to include all of the on costs and you may also wish to include a proportion of any pension deficit of support staff if carrying out the review in an academy.
- The costs of any TLRs (teaching and learning responsibility payments) including on costs.
- The total number of periods available for teaching for each member of staff (normally on a weekly basis).
- The number of periods per week each member of staff spends in direct contact with pupils (in front of class).

- The number of periods per week each member of staff has as non-contact time. It is important that non-contact time is not defined as one category, but it must be broken down into the reasons for non-contact. Some examples of non-contact are PPA (planning, preparation and assessment time), SLT time, management of a particular curriculum area and ECF (early career framework previously known as newly qualified teacher) time.
- A split of the contact and non-contact time broken down per year group and per subject in the case of secondary schools.
- The amount of teaching time the timetable requires in order to operate effectively. This should meet the needs of all pupils including vulnerable pupils and pupils with special educational needs.

Below is a very basic example of a starting point for schools to use to begin to analyse their curriculum delivery structure. The two most important things here are the overall cost and the how the periods are separated between contact and non-contact time. Once the whole curriculum structure has been mapped out like this we can then start to analyse what the data is telling us.

Example

Staff	Point	FTE	TLR	Total cost	Max Teach prd	Contact periods	Non-contact periods	Reason
Name	LD9	1.0		£x		2	8	SLT
Name	UPS3	1.0	TLR	£x		9	1	PPA

I would recommend carrying this out to mirror the school's three year future financial projections and especially if there is a significant change in pupil numbers predicted. The change in pupil numbers may come from mobility of pupils already in school or through the intake years. The years of intake will vary depending on the phase and type of school.

The four pillars of ICFP

Once the initial process of populating the required data has been completed, the four questions every school need to ask are:

- Does the curriculum meet all of the needs of the pupils?
- Does the curriculum comply with the National Curriculum and have accountability measures in place?
- Is the curriculum affordable?
- So basically, is it fit for purpose?

Does one size fit all?

One of the common mistakes we often see when a school undertakes an ICFP review is the number of periods per week (or per fortnight) being used as the base from which to produce calculations. We often see 10 or 25 periods used within a primary setting over the space of a week. In a secondary setting the most commonly used basis is 50 periods over a fortnight or 25 periods per week. This is why it is important a combined approach is taken when completing this exercise. At the very least, the SBL and person in charge of the curriculum should both be involved in the review process where the deployment of staff across the curriculum is planned. The larger the school (especially, secondary, three form plus primary schools and all-through schools) the more important it is to include both people. One without the other rarely works and for a thorough review to be done effectively, both financial management and teaching expertise must be brought together.

Chapter 5

The Building Blocks of ICFP

The big bake off!

Every great cake has quality ingredients which is why it is important for any ICFP exercise to have accurate and up-to-date data feeding into it To put it bluntly, the words I would use are bad cake - poor ingredients - and great cake – good ingredients.

Multiple metrics

There are many metrics which come into play when using ICFP to plan. Due to the many different approaches to ICFP, not all of the metrics are used for each method of calculation but there should be an understanding of what each metric means and how it is calculated. This chapter will focus mainly on what the various metrics mean. Altogether, there are 20 metrics to use within the ICFP framework. Not all of these may be used, but depending on the needs of the school, they all provide a form of intelligence which can be applied to produce an effective ICFP approach to curriculum planning, staff deployment and greater efficiency and effectiveness.

Average class size (ACS)

This is an area which seems straight forward but can be interpreted in different ways. It is also known as the pupil to teacher ratio (PTR) which is applied to the curriculum.

For example, the easiest way to understand this is to take the total number of pupils on roll and divide by the full time equivalent (FTE) number of teachers teaching on the timetable.

If a school has 1500 pupils and the FTE number of teachers teaching is 75, the average class size will be 20. This is a very broad brush approach and is probably best used if you want a figure to compare with other schools. This approach does have some limiting factors:

- It does not take into account the different key stages or year groups. The PTR in year four or year seven will be quite different to the PTR in year 11 and sixth form.
- Does an average approach across the whole school allow direct comparisons with other similar size schools or are there too many factors which could distort some of the micro data?
- It is not a curriculum-led approach to looking at average class size and is better used as a wider benchmark tool, rather than for developing a curriculum-led approach to producing a budget plan.

A curriculum-led approach

When it comes to a curriculum approach to planning a budget, there are 2 schools of thought within the sector. There is the CIPFA approach and the Outwood Grange approach. They work in similar ways with two exceptions of the latter model using a percentage bonus (also known as a relative or curriculum bonus) and being period driven. Most importantly, both of these models put the curriculum first and answer the important questions of what can you do as a school and what you can afford. Regardless of the preferred model, any curriculum structure has to fit within the funding envelope. Any conclusions from this type of approach will no doubt give schools more data to analyse and constructive questions to challenge themselves on, as they seek the optimum model for their school, pupils and finances.

The CIPFA approach

The simplicity of this model makes it the go to calculation due its direct approach to working out the PTR.

The formula PTR = C x ACS

C = Contact ratio

ACS = Average class size

NOR = Number on roll

For a worked scenario we are going to use a secondary school with 1,500 pupils, years 7 – 11. The contact ratio to be used is 0.79. This is the average ratio used by a school when comparing contact time by periods to total number of periods available. The average class size to be used is 25.

PTR = 0.79 x 25 = 19.75

Therefore, for every 19.75 pupils, 1 FTE member of staff would be required to staff the curriculum structure. This is an important figure as it will now be used to calculate the number of teaching staff required by the school to deliver the curriculum.

To calculate the number of teachers required to deliver the curriculum take the number of pupils on roll and divide this by the PTR.

Therefore, 1500/19.75 = 76 FTE teachers

The Outwood Grange approach

I am a big fan of this approach due to its flexibility and bottom up approach in how it develops the needs of the curriculum. It is also the most difficult to initially understand but the most useful and adaptable if the concept can be fully grasped.

Before we look at this it is important to understand how the curriculum bonus works including how and where it can be applied.

Curriculum bonus

Curriculum bonus (or relative bonus) is a weighting term designed to give more flexibility to a curriculum across a school with multiple year groups and phases. When planning a curriculum it is important to establish how many periods would be required to teach or staff each year group. At this stage it is important to consider that each year group is very different and will have varying curriculum needs and a well-planned curriculum will cater for the individual needs of pupils.

If we take year 8 as an example, the number of pupils in each class to aim for would be 27. The figure of 27 is a universally accepted approach in school larger than 700 pupils. The exception to the rule would be schools less than 700 which would normally have 30 pupils per class due to limits on economies of scale and statutory requirements affecting primary schools. Sixth forms would also be exempt and have far smaller classes due how the allocating of the option groups is structured.

Schools which vary the number of pupils in different year groups may have 31 pupils per class in year 7 and 25 pupils per class in year 11.

At the point of having 27 pupils in a class, this would be known as zero curriculum bonus.

If you want classes of 25 pupils, which is 2 less than the 27, this is known as a positive bonus. If the class has 30 pupils in, this would be a negative bonus. The lower the number of pupils in a class, the more periods of teaching would be required because there may be more classes across the year group. The higher the number of pupils in a class, the less periods of teaching would be required because there may be less classes across the year group.

There will be many decisions to make on how a curriculum is structured and the quality or impact a curriculum has will be directly affected by the number of periods which are allocated. Overall, for a school, it may not be a question of how many periods are available, but more of a question of where are those periods allocated in order to give the greatest impact on teaching, learning and wellbeing.

How periods are allocated does have impact on the cost per period and the total costs of teaching staff.

Based on the Outwood Grange model, the trust operates a curriculum bonus of up to 8% to give that opportunity to increase and decrease the number of periods available for teaching in each year group, subject and option. It is not uncommon for schools to operate classes of 31 across multiple year groups in years 7 and 8 so that year 11 has smaller classes.

If the cost per period in a school is £2,200 and 50 periods are deemed surplus to what the curriculum needs, the potential savings will be £110,000 over a year.

This is why it is important to review the non-contact time and different layers of management within the structure. Head teachers will normally have no contact time but we do see in some small schools and one form entry primaries, the head teacher having some contact time. In secondary schools we normally see a split of 22/25 for class based teachers when comparing contact time to overall periods available. For heads of department it is normally a split of 18/25. Assistant heads would have slightly less contact time at 17/25. Deputy head teachers, on average, have a split of 9/25, but the contact time is sometimes significantly higher within primary settings. With the executive head teacher model we have seen some layers of management removed completely from structures with some senior management staff moving back in to full time teaching as schools become more aware and efficient in the use of how non-contact time is utilised and where best to deploy teachers for the maximum impact.

The Outwood Grange approach calculation

The technique uses six main metrics to calculate the total FTE number of teachers to staff the curriculum.

The metrics used are:

P = Periods in a cycle or week (check if this is fortnightly or weekly)

C = Contact ratio

NOR = Number on roll

BCS = Benchmark class size

TL = Teacher load

CB = Curriculum bonus

The two important figures to be used to calculate the number of FTE teachers required to deliver the curriculum are the number of periods and the teacher load. Once we have these figures we can then work out the number of FTE teachers to cost out.

The first thing we are going to work out is the number of periods required.

Number of periods = (NOR/BCS) x P x CB

In this example the number on roll is 1,500 pupils, the benchmark class size is 27 pupils, the number of periods in a cycle is 25 and the curriculum bonus is 8% (for calculation purposes we will use 1.08 as the multiplier).

Number of periods = (1500/27) x 25 x 1.08 = 1,500 periods

This tells us that 1,500 sessions or periods is what is required to be staffed.

The second thing we are going to work out is the teacher load (TL)

TL = P x C

Continuing with the same example, the periods in a cycle remain the same at 25 and the contact ratio is 0.79.

TL = 25 x 0.79 = 19.75

To calculate the number of teachers required to deliver the curriculum take the number of pupils on roll and divide this by the TL.

Therefore, 1500/19.75 = 76 FTE teachers

Just because this calculation tells us the number of teachers required, it does not mean that this is the most cost effective solution for the school. The following will be a number of factors to take into account when seeking the best fit and structure for curriculum delivery:

- The number of staff on the leadership scale.
- How many staff are on TMS (teacher main scale) and UPS (upper pay spine) and how many are towards the top of these scales.
- The number and level of TLRs to be committed.
- Should the level of curriculum bonus be reduced or the contact ratio be increased (by doing this, the number of teachers required would be less as their contact time would increase and the curriculum bonus flexibility would be less).
- Should the contact ratio be decreased or the curriculum bonus increased (assuming it is less than 8% already). This would lead to more teachers being required as the contact time would reduce and there would be more flexibility in the curriculum.

It is important that this is not just used in times of falling roll or fluctuations in funding. This should be the norm and embedded within the school's common practice and used on a regular basis. For example, when a school has planned its curriculum and set its budget, both should be reviewed in line with each other as part of a fully costed school improvement plan. Through careful and consistent monitoring, both pedagogy and financial management should be seen as one even though the curriculum may be the main driver.

All of the approaches are very much driven by the context of the setting. There is no one rule which works across every type of school model but rather, positive elements which can be taken from each approach and used in a multitude of ways to arrive at the curriculum deployment best suited to deliver the most effective and efficient curriculum that can best serve the school community.

'The best approach is a curriculum led approach to staffing rather than a staffing led curriculum.' *Khan, 2021*

Chapter 6

Metrics for Success

'What's measured improves.' *Peter Drucker*

Why do you need quality metrics for your business continuity?

Within school business leadership we often hear the term business continuity. Over the course of the pandemic this has accelerated the way schools approach the continuity of their functions from being able to safely remain open to vulnerable and key worker pupils to offering remote access to online learning.

We rarely see the term business continuity used in the analysis of metrics, but it should as without understanding and using metrics in the correct way, the business continuity of a school could be impeded.

Managed measurement

'If you can manage it, you can measure it.' *Khan, 2021*

The whole concept of metrics is built on being able to measure what you can manage. This gives the ability to control the destiny and direction of any school business. Does your business continuity management program allow for the school's performance to be properly measured? This does not just mean filling in figures for a tick box exercise to seek approval at committee level, but part of the process should be appraising the mid and end-of-year data to ensure you are on track and the financial outcomes are realistic and achievable.

Earlier on, we discussed the value of choosing the right metrics to measure the financial performance of a school. These should be measured regularly as part of Khan's 'Constant' and to evaluate how a school can navigate through its own business continuity and financial disruption. This will highlight any areas which require improvement.

Metrics and KPIs which measure performance and recoverability allow for greater transparency of a school's business including reporting. Through enhanced reporting, there will be more opportunity to receive feedback at committee level so that this can then be used to strategically prioritise where improvements can be made.

The metrics carousel

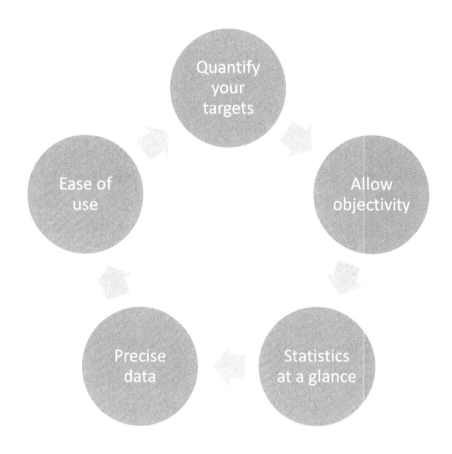

Khan, 2021

As a SBL, senior leadership team or governing body, carrying out an exercise of the Metrics Carousel can enable you to refocus on what the main drivers of your school business are or should be. This is especially useful if a school has falling role, is experiencing a decrease in funding, is experiencing increased costs, or is facing a large or growing in year deficit.

Quantify your targets

The temptation to analyse all of the metrics and KPIs a school can generate from its financial data may seem overwhelming. Just because the school has data on certain areas does not mean it has to all be used. A school may find that it has ten different measurements of financial performance, but it may be that only four of these will bring about any real benefit to the school at that particular moment or in the short to medium term. The real question here is not how many things can be measured, but rather, what should we be quantifying and why. An example may be that the school has a high in year deficit, so the question I would be asking is why and what targets would I want to quantify to enable a strategy to be put in place.

Allow objectivity

Being objective on measurements of financial performance is still fairly new to governing bodies as the critical friend role is normally reserved for questioning around balances, outturns and sustainability of budgets. For objectivity to prevail, there must be an understanding of what financial performance means and how committees can use this data alongside the other statutory reporting requirements. The two are often seen separately but they are really part of the same pie and should be seen as one complementing the other. Objectivity only comes with experience and/or training and it is important for governors to have a deep understanding of how metrics can be used to improve decision making when it comes to budgets.

Statistics (or performance) at a glance

Having data which is readily available to interpret is as important as ease of use. I often see 30 page reports handed out to committees which have pages and pages of information. It may be that only 5% of the report is actually referred to in the meeting with the other 95% not being discussed or may be it is just there for compliance.

My questions for any school are:

- What statistics do you want to show (and do you have too many)?
- How are you showing measurement of performance?

Sometimes it is better to have less information (statistics) accompanying a main finance report as it ensures that more time is being spent on understanding the data to allow better informed decisions to be made.

Precise data

You will be surprised at this approach but having precise data in some circumstances is less important than having the correct methods for calculating metrics. I often see an overreliance on making sure certain costs go to different cost centres, but if the financial controls are well established and strong, this should look after itself. Where schools do become a little stuck sometimes is the way certain metrics are calculated and the extraction of key data. For example when working out the total spend of premises costs as a percentage of overall expenditure, it is easy to miss something off or misunderstand what is being asked.

Ease of use

Any form for financial reporting and comparative data should be easy to use. Its goes back to the 'less is more' rule and having the things you think are important to measure for your school or the particular issue you want to resolve / raise awareness. It is useful to have some metrics or KPIs as standing items on reports so that it is easier to make comparisons throughout the year of a financial cycle. This builds a better understanding of certain measurements and it is always good in introduce new measures gradually, when it is required as a control or when governors become more confident in their interpretation and understanding of the data.

Tops tips - The best mix

What is the best mix of financial measurement data for your school? As a starting point, it is always useful to look back at the historical measures to challenge why these particular measures have been used and what benefits they provide. Having carried out this review at many schools, do not be surprised if up to 40% of your measures change for one reason and one reason only. You may have been measuring the wrong thing or you may not have included the correct amounts in the calculation. This is a common problem but easily rectified.

Chapter 7

Measurable Metrics

Average teacher cost (ATC)

This metric is very under used but is particularly useful in large MATs when comparing the ATC across a range of schools, especially schools which may be new to a MAT. It is also a useful indicator to use in standalone schools over a period of time so that trends in the average can be analysed.

As teaching staff take up the largest percentage of any budget within the overall staffing and as a whole, this is a metric which should be broken down so that schools understand the significance of their data. This ATC is a key element in understanding the amount of money being spent on teaching staff as well as the total FTE number of teachers within the school's workforce.

The calculation for the ATC is:

Total spend of teaching staff / FTE number of teachers

The total spend should include all responsibility points and members of the leadership team. Any HLTAs should be taken out of the calculation at this point, but used in any narrative accompanying the ATC data. Only teaching staff directly on the schools payroll should be included in the ATC with supply staff not to be used in the calculation.

The more supply staff who are teaching at the school, the lower the relevance of the ATC metric. It is always important to explain any context behind the figure as it may cause distortion within the data if it is not fully representative of a full staffing complement.

For the majority of financial metrics in schools, there is nationally recognised threshold data. Comparing each school's data is the first step to benchmarking against similar types of school.

If the ATC is higher than the average, this may be due to:

- A senior (age) or experienced staffing structure
- A higher or historic level of TLRs being awarded
- A higher probability of awarding increments in pay through performance management
- A higher proportion of staff on the leadership spine

If the ATC is lower than the average, this may be due to:

- A more junior (age) or inexperienced staffing structure
- Not many TLRs being awarded
- More rigorous performance management process where it is harder to increment through the pay scales
- A lower proportion of staff on the leadership spine

Data from the Education Policy Institute (EPI) found that between 2002 and 2017 per pupil spending increased by 42% but per pupil expenditure on teachers only increased by 17%. This would support the notion of an increase in spend on other areas such as teaching assistants and back office staff.

The EPI has also done some research on the spending patterns of secondary schools that joined large MATs between 2003 and 2010 and how spend has changed over time between 2010 and 2017. It was found that there were large reductions in spend post joining the MAT with large fluctuations in their pupil teacher ratio (PTR). This could point towards a change in how teachers in the school and across the trust have been deployed and a shift in the approach the MAT has taken towards workforce management.

Benchmark class size

This is also known as the average class size and is used to universally compare the average size of a class between schools with differing timetable cycles.

There has been a lot of research carried out into the effects of class sizes in schools and the impact this has on the business as a whole including the pupils.

The name used within ICFP circles is the pupil teacher ratio and you can see why it is the preferred benchmark for school to school comparisons. Previously, we saw how to calculate the PTR by taking the total number of pupils and dividing the figure by the total FTE number of teachers.

A more bespoke approach would be to use a method which takes into account how a school deploys it teaching staff over individual year groups to deliver more individual requirements to pupils and to show how requirements by key stage influence the average class size by year group.

One of the most common myths is when you decrease the average class size it has a positive impact on pupil attainment. Extensive research has been carried out in the US where class sizes have had an impact on attainment levels, especially if the class size is reduced below 18 pupils and this has been sustained for at least 3 years. There is also evidence in the UK, within deprived primary settings, that there is a positive impact on pupils who are in classes of less than 20 pupils.

The Education Endowment Foundation (EEF) has carried out research into the strategies which impact on pupil progress, and, on average, reducing class sizes has an impact of three months additional progress for pupils.

Reducing class sizes can be misleading in what one would expect the outcomes to be. Automatically, you would expect improvement within the process of teaching and learning, an increase in the amount of high quality feedback, and more one-to-one time with pupils. The evidence does show that these improvements do not occur until there is a substantial reduction in class size to less than 20 or even 15 pupils.

There would be 2 main reasons for reducing class size, being, does it allow greater flexibility within other year groups to allow smaller classes and reduce overall spend within the budget? The two are directly related to each other. If a class was being reduced from 29 to 25, the research does not support a proportionate impact on attainment at this level.

Reduced class sizes

Below is a table summarising some EEF findings on reduced class sizes:

Reduced class size	Advantages	Disadvantages
	New approach to teaching can increase attainment.	Same teacher approach as before may not have an impact on attainment.
	Benefits on attainment can be identified.	Risk of loss of consistency due to additional staff required.
	More focused positive impact occurs in primary schools, lower prior attainment pupils and disadvantaged pupils.	Increase in costs. If a class of 30 pupils is split into 2 classes of 15 pupils, the additional teaching cost per pupil is around £1,150.
	If CPD is focused on teaching skills and approaches, there are benefits to attainment,	

	behaviour and attitude.	

The most important take-away from this is not 'how do we reduce class sizes?', but how do we change the way we deploy staff so that smaller groups have more intensive teaching or teaching assistant time?

Cost of one lesson

The cost of one lesson is being used more and more as an internal financial control mechanism rather than a figure to benchmark against other schools with.

It is one of the simplest metrics to calculate, but is still underused as its significance is underrated and misunderstood, due to the limited availability of examples.

The two important figures to use to calculate the cost of one lesson are the total teaching staff costs and the maximum teaching periods available per week over a year. The teaching periods per week may be 10 or 25 depending on how the school plans its curriculum and deploys its staff. I would always recommend converting the total number of periods available to a basis of 25. For example, if you are using 10 periods per week, you would need to multiply by 2.5.

Cost of one lesson = Total teaching staff costs / maximum number of periods available

In this example the total teaching staff costs are £1,100,000 and the maximum number of periods available are 550 per week. The number of periods in a cycle is 25 but we will not be using this figure as it has already been used in calculating the number of periods available.

Cost of one lesson = £1,100,000 / 550 = £2,000 per lesson

The reason this figure is important from a budget planning perspective is because it enables capacity to be quantified into monetary terms. Its use in primary schools is limited, but it should be part of the staple metrics used in secondary schools as it is a quick way of totalling the cost benefit of allocating additional periods or reducing them across multiple year groups. I have also seen fluctuations in the cost of one lesson ranging from, £1,900 to £2,200. The cost in each school is whatever it is and is an excellent measure of financial cost across MATS. In order to measure the financial value and efficiency of the cost of one lesson, you would need to standardise how you are measuring both value and efficiency by agreeing what educational outcomes you would be measuring, for example, attainment, progress, or wellbeing.

Pupil numbers (as a metric and non-metric)

As budgets become tighter, more emphasis is placed upon the pupil number data to seek trends in overall numbers for future years and the make up for the different pupil-led elements of the funding formula. The overall increase in pupils within the state sector between 2015 and 2019 was 3.9% with the rate of increase tapering off from 2017. This gradual reduction in the rate of increase in pupil numbers looks set to become negative by 2024 as the impact of Brexit and the pandemic converge to produce a steep decrease in birth rates, possibly up to 20% based on the birth data coming out of Italy and France in January 2021.

This places greater attention on what is behind local fluctuations (trends in local pupil numbers may not follow national or regional trends as there will be other factors like proximity, popularity and catchment areas) in pupil numbers and what the socio demographics of the pupil population are made up of.

The primary sector is facing the more imminent challenge as numbers reduce sharply from 2022 and intakes become leaner. The secondary sector is well insulated until 2025, and then there will be sharp declines in intakes as the admissions become more impacted by the overall picture in primary schools.

Since 2018, the percentage of pupils eligible for FSM (free school meals) in all schools has increased sharply from 13.6% in 2018 to 15.4% in 2019 to 17.3% in 2020. Since April 2018, transitional protections have been in place which will continue to be in place during the roll out of Universal Credit. This has meant that pupils eligible for free school meals on or after 1

April 2018 retain their free school meals eligibility even if their circumstances change. This has been the main driver in the increase in the proportion of pupils eligible for free school meals as pupils continue to become eligible but fewer pupils stop being eligible.

Due to the increases in the overall percentage of FSM pupils in some schools, there may be some impact on the financial benchmarking comparison data and the resource management threshold data ratings which may push a previously low FSM school into a medium FSM category or a previously medium FSM school into a high FSM category. This is especially important when comparing different years of data as the financial benchmarking may select different schools to those previously selected, based on characteristics.

Pupil premium is an area which can get overlooked and bringing its calculation in line with the October census date should make things easier to predict despite the controversial change in methodology from January 2021 to October 2020. The change in date to October will also put more pressure on schools to scoop up any outstanding eligibility towards the start of the academic year.

We previously covered the potential cost of splitting classes but it may mean we sees things going the other way with larger classes and a hybrid model of learning off shooting from the national lockdowns and the online learning platforms available.

It is vital that schools project their pupil numbers, including characteristics of the numbers and how individual year groups may be affected. This more detailed approach to predicting funding will support the longer term projections of funding but also metrics and KPIs. In mixed MATS, this will become even more important and due to the shift in pupil number growth from primary to secondary over the next five years, the deployment of staff to resource the curriculum may see more cross-phase movement of staff between primary and secondary. This is something we already see in all-through schools.

Periods per week

The number of periods or sessions per week will vary depending on the type of school. The most common split used within the secondary sector is a fortnightly 50 period split where five periods are allocated per day over ten days. Some primary schools use a weekly ten period cycle to plan their curriculum. Some deployment models in secondary use a 60 period split over a fortnight but this is rare. When a school uses the fortnightly split, the periods per week can be different.

Pupil to adult ratio

The pupil to adult ratio is slightly subjective and dependent on the data schools decide to include in their calculation. There is room for two interpretations of the ratio and how it can be calculated and more importantly, used. This ratio is used as an indicator of how many pupils there are in a school to each FTE member of staff.

To calculate the pupil to adult ratio:

Pupil to adult ratio = total number of pupils divided by FTE total school workforce

There is also a direct contact pupil to curriculum staff ratio:

Direct contact pupil to curriculum staff ratio = total number of pupils divided by FTE total curriculum staff

The universally used calculation is the former, but the second method provides more of an insight into the direct relationship between pupil numbers and all staff involved in the curriculum. The benefit of using all curriculum staff is that it moderates any impact back office or other support staff may have on the ratio. This is particularly useful in PFI (private finance initiative) schools and schools which outsource support staff.

If a school has a high pupil to adult ratio, the class sizes may be larger than normal, the teaching workload may be greater than normal and there may be a negative impact on the outcomes of pupils. If a school has a low pupil to adult ratio, the class sizes may be smaller compared to the average and there may be higher staffing costs due to more FTE staff deployed across the workforce relative to the total number of pupils.

Pupil to teacher ratio

The pupil to teacher ratio can be calculated in more than one way but the general approach differs from some of the approaches covered earlier.

To calculate the pupil to teacher ratio:

Pupil to teacher ratio = total number of pupils divided by FTE total teaching staff

One of the advantages of this calculation is that it takes values where there is little room for error or manipulation. For example, to standardise the comparison between different schools the FTE teaching staff should include any supply vacancies otherwise the PTR could be distorted. A disadvantage of using the calculation is that it does not show the impact on individual classes and the school may have 15 pupils in some classes and 30 in others. For a deeper understanding of the PTR in secondary schools, it may be useful to carry out the analysis per key stage or even year group. This would provide more context to the broader calculation of the whole school.

We tend to only analyse this figure, but the real benefit comes if it is used to manage workload and class sizes. This would be especially useful in year groups where there is over capacity where the number of pupils is reducing but the FTE number of teaching staff is remaining the same. The deployment of the workforce should be shaped by curriculum demand, hence curriculum-led.

Senior leaders' workforce ratio

This ratio can be used in two ways as there are two separate calculations which can be derived from this method. This is a useful ratio which becomes powerful within MATs, in particular those MATs which are conducting due diligence on schools which are interested in joining a trust.

The first calculation is the senior leader workforce ratio and the denominator is the total FTE workforce including all support services such as catering and cleaning.

To calculate the senior leader workforce ratio:

Senior leader workforce ratio = total FTE senior leaders divided by FTE total school workforce

The second calculation is the senior leader teaching workforce ratio.

To calculate the senior leader teaching workforce ratio:

Senior leader teaching workforce ratio = total FTE senior leaders divided by FTE total teaching staff workforce

Both of these calculations will measure different aspects of the workforce, but if the ratio is too high, it could signal a top heavy leadership structure or a possible low teacher contact ratio due to higher non-contact time.

It is important to emphasise that any one particular ratio may not be enough on its own and should be used in conjunction with other metrics to show a fuller picture of financial and workforce measurement.

Teacher contact ratio

The teacher contact ratio is one of the underpinning metrics of ICFP and originally started being used in a different form many years ago and was commonly known as the average teaching load (ATL). This is the average number of periods per FTE teacher.

To calculate the average teacher load:

Average teacher load = Total number of contact periods divided by total FTE number of teachers

For example, if a school has a 50 period timetable cycle over a fortnight and has 60 FTE teachers, the total number of periods available is 3,000. If out of the 3,000 periods available, 2,300 of the periods are classed as direct contact periods, the ATL is:

ATL = 2,300 / 60 = 38.33 periods

On this calculation, you could conclude that the contact ratio is 0.77 (38.33 / 50).

There is nothing wrong with using the ATL to plan and analyse a school curriculum using this basis, but it does become a little unstable if a comparison is being made with another schools ATL as it only works if the base number of periods in the timetable are identical. For example, you would not be able to compare the ATL between a school that has 50 periods in its cycle and a school that has 40 or 45 periods.

This is why the contact ratio becomes the focus of not only how a school should calculate average contact time, but how a school compares itself with other schools and national benchmarks.

The contact ratio of 0.78 was first explored by Sam Ellis, in 2008, when a question was asked, 'what should the contact ratio be?'. The official response became known as the ASCL level and is broken down by the following:

- 100% is be classed as the total time available.
- 10% is available for PPA time.
- 10% is available for management time.
- 2% for any margin of error.
- The net total of direct contact time is 78% or a contact ratio of 0.78.

There is no rule to say that the contact ratio should be 0.78, but with statutory PPA time and management time required, it gives little wriggle room to manoeuvre, especially in schools of less than 400 pupils. The larger the school, the more useful this mechanism becomes in being able to adapt curriculum delivery and support for pupils.

The contact ratio should not be the same in each school and the there is a balance to be struck between the needs of the curriculum and the wellbeing of pupils (this is especially important in a post pandemic world). It is important for anyone planning a timetable to have comparative data to measure against and 0.78 as a contact ratio is probably the closest measure of what a curriculum can look like (note not should look like). Following an increase in online teaching and learning, we may see the shape of curriculum delivery change dramatically to direct contact and virtual contact ratios. This is now a distinct possibility. The person planning the timetable should have the ability to increase flexibility within individual contact time for teaching depending upon the pedagogy and pastoral demands. Just because there is a benchmark, it does not mean you have to stick to it.

The contact ratio is another great metric to compare schools within the same trust or locally between single schools. Personally, I like to use it as challenge tool. If a school has a low contact ratio, there may be some inefficiency within the structure or there may be a valid reason for having it at such a level. Two questions to support the evaluation of a contact ratio are how sustainable is it and how much would changing the contact ratio by one percent cost. If it can be quantified into monetary terms, it can be planned within a structure, a budget and used to consider or justify making savings.

Teacher support staff ratio

The teacher support staff ratio is not a commonly known metric used in schools. On its own, it can give a good indicator of the makeup of the workforce and if there is an over reliance of support staff within a schools' structure.

It is one of the only ratios used within the financial management of schools which can be below one and above one.

The formula for calculating the teacher support staff (TSR) ratio is:

Teacher support staff ratio = FTE number of teacher / FTE number of support staff

For example, if the FTE number of teachers is 18 and the FTE number of support staff is 20, the teacher support ratio would be:

$$TSR = 18 / 20 = 0.90$$

Another example is if the FTE number of teachers is 21 and the FTE number of support staff is 20, the teacher support ratio would be:

TSR = 21 / 20 = 1.05

These two different ratio calculations may also indicate differences in the teacher contact ratio. If the TSR is below one, this may be because the teacher contact ratio is high. This could mean a low number of FTE teachers in the structure which may lead to an increase in overall contact time.

If the TSR is above one, this may be because the teacher contact ratio is low. This would mean a high number of FTE teachers in the structure which may lead to a decrease in overall contact time.

The reason it is important to take into account other ratios and factors is because the TSR does not provide enough data initially. As an efficiency tool, the best metrics to use alongside the TSR are the teacher contact ratio and the progress scores by subject.

The three of these combined will give a greater understanding of the following:

- How a workforce is structured.
- Which areas of staffing have targeted investment.
- The delivery structure of teaching and pastoral support.

- Which priority areas of staffing having the biggest impact on progress.
- Where the best areas to invest are.
- How efficient the delivery of the curriculum is.
- If there is over capacity within the existing structure.
- How the TSR look across schools in the same trust.
- What the average TSR look like in a trust.

This is another very quick due diligence checker when trusts are carrying out full HR and financial reviews on potential new schools which may be joining the trust.

If a school is predicting in year deficits in the future, the TSR can be used along with the metrics which complement and support this data. When making a case for any change in the staffing structure, the more useful metrics which can be used, the stronger the case will be and the more likely it is that it will stand up to scrutiny.

Tops tips – Combine your data

There are several useful metrics which can be used to measure financial performance, and there will be some used more than others due to their value to the school and in how useful they are in breaking down data as well as keeping you on track. We previously explored the reliance of the sector on box ticking and compliance when assessing performance. In order to achieve the highest level of understanding from your financial metric data, it will be essential that several sets of data are analysed because they will most likely influence each other and it is vital that correlations in data are fully understood. Combining your data and looking at it holistically will give a greater understanding of what the main drivers are and which areas are most at risk.

Chapter 8

KPI Vitals

Measuring the right things

This is the same question Formula One teams constantly ask of themselves in a sport of fine margins. The same philosophy can also be applied to financial management and the measurement of financial performance in schools. If you were running a Formula One team, which measurements of performance would you use and why?

The first question you should be looking to answer is not what should I be using, but what are you trying to achieve. Without this basic understanding of intent, you could become a slave to statistics, when it should be the statistics driving your performance.

How do you drive performance?

It is important to define as accurately as possible what a winning performance will look like. We often see the prescribed lists of DfE measures without realising which ones are the most valid and require the most attention. To be crude, which ones give the biggest impact and will serve the school best.

Much of the focus of KPIs is placed on a completed financial year's worth of data, or in the event of predicting KPIs it is most commonly used to measure a 12 month period. This is where Formula One has the advantage over other sectors as it breaks down performance per lap and does not entirely view performance as a completed race. This is where measuring a school's financial performance could be measured if it was broke down to KPIs per month or even each term. I can see this working well with measuring supply and some of the core KPI measures. The education sector has become conditioned to only look at KPI data once the event (or year) has been completed. In the context of a Formula One race, you cannot manage the team's performance on a KPI result because it only becomes available once the race has been completed. Therefore, we do need to change the way we see KPI data in both, what type of data is the most effective for measuring performance and how often should we consider using this data and its overall purpose to the school's vision.

To help support the sound financial measurement of performance, it is important to establish a charter to align the aims of the team. The team should extend to the whole school, as ultimately, budget holders will be operating at varying levels. It is important that staff feel empowered enough to feel a part of the decision making process as this is likely to drive behaviours such as seeking value for money.

The financial performance charter

Khan, 2021

The financial performance charter (FPC) combines characteristics of elite sport and business to show how leadership can drive behaviour in making financial decisions but its underlying purpose is to empower staff to make the best decisions possible in the strategic interest of the school and its overall vision. KPIs should be a part of this as they will help drive the financial performance keeping it closely aligned with the school improvement plan.

The first step is to establish the leadership system to hold different people to account and this starts at both the top and bottom, as the main aim is to empower the school's budget holders (decision makers) to make decisions which will support the school's vision as well as allow financial discipline to be aligned to the school's financial KPIs.

Once the responsibilities for the team have been determined, to allow fluid feedback to accountability in step one, the next stage will be to communicate what you want to achieve and how this may drive positive financial behaviour. The behaviour and values should also be in line with the school's overall vision.

Through delegation of budgets to staff, it is important to allow staff enough freedom to make spending decisions as long as it is within the budget envelope. This will allow staff to buy in to the collective vision, as well as feel empowered by SLT to make decisions on spend.

The level of delegation will determine how much budget responsibility staff members have. There will be large differences between how different types of schools operate within the FPC. The FPC for a standalone school may look different to the FPC of a school within a MAT, with the level of autonomy being a factor which may differ considerably. I know within some large MATs the levels of financial autonomy are restricted at individual school level with the vast majority of decisions made at central trust level. I can see both the advantages and disadvantages of this.

What to measure and why

One of the areas SBLs can get stuck on is what is the right set or complement of financial measures to use and when is best to use them. I often see prescribed lists of measures with little thought given to, whether it is actually useful and will it benefit my school. My advice would be that it depends on both the context and position the school finds itself in. There is no one-size-fits-all where metrics and KPIs are concerned but it is more about having the right mix of measures, which are going to tell you the most about what is going on within the school's financial reports or balance sheet.

It is amazing how many schools fall at the first hurdle in not understanding what financial values are required to be included in the different measures available.

Total Staff Costs as % of Total Revenue Income

This is one of the most widely used KPIs but I very rarely see it used in the correct way. There is a chasm in the methodology used to calculate the value, with the main error caused when deciding what staff costs to include in the calculation. The reason this percentage is heavily relied on is because it is easy to compare against local, national, similar type and size school benchmarks, but it is also defines a split between staffing costs and non-staffing costs.

Below is an example of the staffing areas to include in the calculation, which includes all on costs for all staff on the schools payroll. Special consideration should be used in the rate applied to the support staff employers' pension contribution if calculating on costs for schools in a MAT:

- Teaching staff.
- Administration staff.
- Teaching assistants.
- Building services supervisor.
- Other curriculum support staff.
- Midday supervisors.
- Cleaners.
- Catering staff.
- Staff on maternity leave.
- Staff on sick leave.

It is important to note that supply staff are not included within this calculation but should be used in a separate calculation of their own.

The two areas, which should be clarified as this is where the most confusion arises, are what happens if the school contracts out its cleaning or catering.

The two are treated very differently when it comes to including these costs in the main KPI calculation.

If a school contracts out its cleaning, the school should use 90% of the value of the overall cleaning contract. For example, if the cleaning contract is worth £30,000, the value to be used in the

KPI calculation will be £27,000. The other 10% is accounted for by cleaning materials and is not included in the staffing costs.

If the school contracts out its catering provision, the school should use 50% of the value of the overall catering contract. This assumes that the catering staff are not directly employed by the school but by the catering company. For example, if the catering contract is worth £100,000, the value to be used in the KPI calculation will be £50,000. The other 50% is accounted for by food / other provision costs and is not included in the staffing costs. If the catering provider uses agency staff in the event of a vacancy, this cost is to be included in the staffing costs.

The calculation for Total Staff Costs as % of Total Revenue Income is:

Total spend on staff / Total revenue income

The total revenue income should include all sources of income the school receives including government funding and other external income such as income from lettings and school meals income. Capital funding should be excluded from the calculation. If the school has significant trading entities which generate income (teaching school or research school), due care must be taken when deciding whether to include this as it could distort the percentage. Any surplus balances brought forward from the previous financial year are excluded from the calculation.

An example of the total staff costs as % of total revenue income is below:

If a school has total staff costs of £1.72m and the overall funding and income is £2m the calculation would be as follows:

Total staff costs as % of total revenue income = (1.72 / 2) x 100 = 86%

With any KPI data, there are of course caveats. If this analysis is being done across a MAT, the question should be asked of what constitutes staffing within the central MAT. It is important to take into account the full staffing costs, not only at individual school level but at central level to as the latter could reduce the individual KPI at school level if it is not considered within the context of the overall data. There is a school of thought that any central MAT staff costs should be apportioned between the individual schools, but that is an entirely different conversation, with so many possible recharge permutations of how this could be calculated and how do you consider what is fair when deciding the basis to use in working out the KPI.

Where is the sweet spot?

There have been lots of debates during my long career in school business management and the figures I hear banded around the most are 80% and most recently 75%. So where do these figures come from? The historic 80% was first used by Ofsted back in the late 1990s when full budget delegation took effect and schools were given full control of their budgets and spending. This figure held steady during the Labour government between 1997 and 2010. When the first pupil premium allocations were given to schools in 2012 the dynamics of the percentage changed to around 78% and this figure has held ever since. One of the main problems which has arisen is that pay awards have not necessarily been fully funded through the national funding formula and this is applying stress on the 78% benchmark. We initially saw this just before the teachers' pay grant and teachers' pension grant were temporarily introduced as separate funding streams back in 2019 (included within the main funding statement from 2021 with the exception of nurseries which will see this as a separate funding stream as before). My thoughts are that if pupil numbers continue at the current rate of decline, the stress on this particular KPI will push more schools to become part of a MAT so that they can centralise more back office support and seek more economies of scale from the restructuring of the school and the MATs leadership structure. The challenge is more imminent within the primary sector and the current dips in birth rate will not be fully felt within the secondary sector until 2025.

Total Teaching Staff Costs as % of Total Revenue Income

This very useful KPI has really come to prominence over the last two years as more and more national benchmarking data, especially around the different types of characteristics of schools, has become widely accessible. The national benchmark for this data for different types of school has crept up gradually over the last few years, mainly down to cost increases outside of the control of schools.

The calculation for Total Teaching Staff Costs as % of Total Revenue Income is:

Total spend on teaching staff / Total revenue income

The total teaching staff costs should include all teaching staff, including senior leaders, and any teaching and learning responsibility points. If the school employs HLTAs for the delivery of lessons (no more than 60% of the HLTAs time), this should also be included in the calculation under teaching staff costs. If this were left out the school could be under reporting the actual KPI percentage and this may not tie up with the teacher contact ratio data. The teacher contact ratio and the total teaching staff costs as % of total revenue income are interrelated as the two should be individually benchmarked and then scrutinised to see if one outcome supports the other. For example, does having a high total teaching staff cost as % of total revenue income ratio mean that the school has too many staff (high FTE) or too many staff who are paid towards the top of their salary scale. The two are very different, which is why the context of the teaching staff structure should always be dissected along with using ICFP data to see what links between the two data sets can be found.

An example of the total teaching staff costs as % of total revenue income is below:

If a school has total teaching staff costs of £1.1m and the overall funding and income is £2m the calculation would be as follows:

Total teaching staff costs as % of total revenue income = (1.1 / 2) x 100 = 55%

This figure is quite high compared to national benchmarks of between 46% and 48% and the teacher contact ratio in this case could be too low with a larger than normal percentage of staff having non-contact time. My first port of call in this case would be to examine the non-contact time, level of pay and the number of teaching staff employed by the school. KPIs are only as good as the data fed into them and it comes back to which KPI mix is best for your school (see performance measurement sheet). You do not need to use every single KPI or metric.

Leadership (and Management) Costs as % of Overall workforce

Out of all the KPIs available this is the least used in schools and is not utilised to its full potential as it often becomes confused with management costs. Further to this there are conflicts between LA compliance requirements, academy KPIs and DfE reporting guidance on what data is the most useful.

I have seen many different formulas used to measure leadership costs which also include using FTE as a basis and compare the leadership cost to overall expenditure. One of the main problems with these comparisons is that there are more anomalies which could skew the data as schools may not be consistent in their approach in what is included. For example if a school were to compare the leadership FTE to the overall teaching staff FTE, it will produce one set of data to compare against other schools but without knowing the individual circumstances of the comparison schools, this data could be seen as less reliable. The leadership costs could be compared to the overall expenditure, but again, there are other variables which can distort this data such as exceptional spend and the extent of any in-year deficit.

The definition of what should be included within any calculation for leadership costs also leads to another question of how do we account for the management costs when deciding on how to use this KPI?

The definitions of leadership costs is:

Any member of staff who is on the leadership spine or/and is on the senior leadership team (in 99% of cases the member of staff will be on the leadership spine). Any support staff should be excluded from this calculation even if they are paid on the leadership spine).

The definition of management costs is:

Any member of staff who is on the leadership spine or/and is on the senior leadership team plus the value of any TLRs including the respective oncosts.

This will provided two KPI figures to use and compare with other schools. The first will compare leadership costs as a percentage of overall workforce and the second will compare management costs as a percentage of overall workforce.

The second KPI is particularly useful in secondary schools but I would calculate both because it is important to examine the gearing between the two especially in the event of falling roll or a restructure. This is a great tool to use across a MAT and when carrying due diligence reviews prior to academisation, as it will highlight inefficiencies and will make it easier to prioritise where to invest within the staffing. These KPIs are can be used within the different and emerging specialisms within the SBL sphere such as HR.

The calculation for Leadership Costs as % of Overall workforce is:

Leadership costs / Total cost of workforce

The calculation for Management Costs as % of Overall workforce is:

Management costs / Total cost of workforce

An example of the leadership costs as % of overall workforce is below:

If a school has leadership costs of £300K and the overall workforce cost is £1.7m the calculation would be as follows:

Leadership costs / Total cost of workforce = (0.3 / 1.7) x 100 = 17.64%

Leadership FTE as % of Overall workforce

Now, let's use a different basis where we work out a similar equation but use the FTE instead of the costs.

If a school has a leadership FTE of 3.8 and the overall workforce FTE is 43, the leadership FTE as a % of overall workforce FTE is 8.84%

These are two similar types of methodology, but provide two very different sets of data The first set of data measures the financial ratio of leadership costs and the second measures the FTE ratio of leadership FTE.

Leadership Efficiency Gearing (LEG)

Both of the percentage figures calculated can be used to measure leadership gearing within individual schools, especially in academy trusts.

For example, taking the two data sets in the above section, if we divide one by the other we can calculate a leadership efficiency gearing (LEG) which can be compared from school to school.

The calculation for Leadership gearing is:

Leadership FTE as % of Overall workforce FTE / Leadership Costs as % of Overall workforce = 8.84 / 17.64 = 0.50

The reason this is important is because the LEG is an indicator of the leadership FTE relative to the leadership costs and it can be used within academy trusts to benchmark schools but it can assist in the deployment of leadership staff. It is a different layer to ICFP which is curriculum lead rather than workforce (this is also dependent on the size of school). I do not think there is such a thing as an ideal national benchmark for this as this is new critical thinking in this area, but on testing over a range of schools, 0.50 seems to be a LEG figure which was common.

Below is a table which explains how a schools LEG can be analysed:

LEG value of 0.50 to be taken as average or the average value within the Trust		
LEG Value	Reason (%FTE)	Reason (%Workforce)
High gearing (above 0.50)	FTE could be too high	Leadership costs could be too low
Low gearing (below 0.50)	FTE could be too low	Leadership costs could be too high

When carrying out a restructure and developing a business case, this data will become very important as it can be used to build the case for reprioritising costs or moving personnel around within a trust.

The LEG is also another set of data which can be combined with the teacher contact ratio, especially if there is a low teacher contact ratio, a significant in year deficit and / or falling pupil numbers.

Other staffing areas as % of Overall workforce

This is an area which does not get used as much as it should and it is an excellent measure, especially against national data and internal trust data. The calculations work in the same way as the comparison for teaching staff costs and are excellent for checking the KPI of individual areas such as administration staff and curriculum support staff. These are key KPIs to use in the event of falling pupil numbers and a restructure.

Total Staff Costs as % of in year expenditure

If there is a KPI which can tell you the most about your staffing costs, this is it. Its simplicity make it a go-to-comparator, but most SBLs make the mistake of only looking at this as a measurement of staffing when they should also be looking at this data alongside the total staff costs as % total revenue income.

If a school only measures against it's in year expenditure, there may be exceptional spend within the year which distorts the result. This may be due to a one off significant purchase. This would need to be reported separately at board level due to its impact on the KPIs and the amount.

The current national data available shows that the average staffing costs as % of in year expenditure is 72% in a primary school and 73% in both secondary schools and MATs. In a MAT you are more likely to see a range of averages depending on the cost base and overall income and expenditure.

Chapter 9

The CFO Charter

'Hunker down and learn something difficult.'

Robin Washington

From present to future

At the beginning of the book we explored the way in which we needed to change when it came to viewing data within the business of education. Through the various chapters we have dived deep in to the analytical areas and skills required to produce a broader understanding of financial intelligence within schools.

We also started with a core mantra for how school business leadership was evolving in stating that the progression of how we apply our knowledge is the natural evolution of any profession.

We could say that school business leadership has always been there in some form, but it has not always been visible until the last 15 years. We are now seeing another large metamorphosis of the profession in the chief financial officer (CFO) role and this role is seismic as it puts the CFO role directly on par with the chief executive officer (CEO) role.

These two pathways are very defined within the private sector, but the jump from school business manager, operations manager or finance manager to CFO is not a well-defined pathway with the skill set required for the role, being a significant step up from the regular school business management competencies.

The CFO Charter

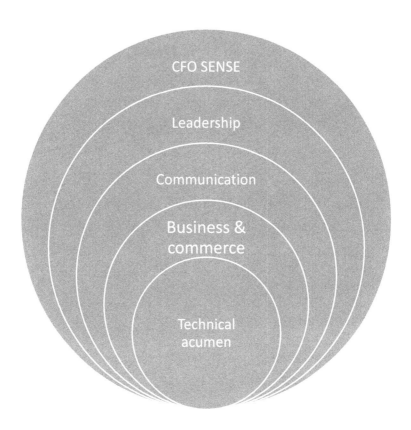

The CFO charter is a list of key pillars which underpin the multitude of competencies required to successfully carry out the role of CFO. Some competencies will cross more than one pillar, which is why the charter is brief but the variety of competencies supported by the pillars is more descriptive. This is a progressive model, rather than a descriptive model set in stone, as it relies on core foundation knowledge for each area, but is surrounded by high level emotional intelligence which is a key element to the CFO role and charter.

Technical acumen

An effective CFO has excellent financial skills crafted through both professional development and experience at a senior level of the organisation. It is important to understand the way accounting standards apply to the school business, especially when things are changing in a sector driven by compliance and financial performance. The CFO does not always need to be the technical lead and as long as there is someone who is proficient in this area, the CFO can spend more time overseeing the running of the business. If you have not got the skill set within your organisation, buy it in!

Business and commerce

Awareness of the entire school business, at every level, both internally and externally, is an essential aspect of any CFO role. The strategic overview of business direction, the scope for opportunities and impact of external influences are all areas which the CFO will need to harness in order to take advantage of changes whilst growing, improving and protecting the school business.

Communication

The CFO will be an important influencer across the business and requires a multitude of skills to communicate at various levels within the business. This is one of the key areas, due to the need to communicate complex issues to a variety of audiences, as stakeholders demand accurate information and transparency in real time.

Leadership

Surprisingly, this is where the CFO should spend the majority of their time. School business managers, at most, spend 10 to 20% of their time within the leadership sphere. CFOs have in the past spent much of their time working on financial reporting, compliance and delivering reports. Today's CFO in schools needs to be able to see the bigger picture and should be able to lead with agility and advanced decision making. The emerging CFO model in schools will eventually see the role turned on its head with up to 50% of their time spent on leadership.

CFO SENSE

CFO SENSE is a key psychological area which is partly science-led and is more centred on the non-visible skills of a CFO. These skills are important as they are tools which allow the other four pillars to function properly. They also surround the pillars as they act as both the glue and the driver of change. I often see the words 'catalyst for change' being used, but an effective CFO should embed change in their organisation so that it becomes a part of the overall culture.

Soft Skills (S)

Coming from a corporate background, it is often the hard skills which become dominant as these tend to be the skills used the most in running day-to-day operations. It is easy to neglect soft skills but these are the skills likely to be the new dominant in a post-Covid era. Examples of soft skills would be negotiating, building morale, communication and building relationships.

Emotional intelligence (E)

This an important area within CFO SENSE and the most difficult to master. From my own experience it cannot be taught academically but should be learnt through experience and emotion. In order to bring out the best in other people within your organisation, you first need to learn to bring out the best in yourself. This is why it is important to understand self-awareness, how your behaviour is perceived and how it impacts on the organisation including its people.

Neuroleadership (N)

Neuroleadership is commonly used within teaching practice to support pupil learning but it is not used extensively by leaders to make their organisations run more effectively. Neuroleadership is an effective strategy which combines scientific research with business practices to help CFOs create and embed behaviour change across the entire organisation.

Self-motivation (S)

This is the bread and butter of leadership and is an essential skill for a CFO. With intelligent leadership, it is the catalyst which ignites most other leadership skills and is preceded by a genuine passion for continuous improvement and positive change. It is also about knowing your limits so that you do not suffer from burnout which will enable you to manage your productivity better.

Entrepreneurship (E)

Over the last five years we have seen the commercial sector evolve the CFO role even further with some global companies such as Twitter and Grubhub, absorbing the chief operating officer (COO) role within the CFO role. This is something we are seeing with the education sector with CFOs required to focus on more than just finance. It is my belief that we are five to ten years away from CFO salaries becoming on par with that of CEOs. In a fast-moving sector where nothing stands still, an effective CFO should be constantly scanning the horizons for commercial opportunities, whether, externally or internally within the academy trust, and any potential partners or potential trust schools. As more challenges outside the financial realm arise, the CFO should be ready to exploit any opportunities which may present themselves.

Chapter 10

The CFO Competency Framework

The days of future past

Back in 2017, I designed and delivered an executive leaders training programme to a group of medium to large sized MATs who were all planning to grow. There was a mixture of SBMs, FDs, executive head teachers, head teachers and CEOs. The skills sets varied a lot due to the diversity of the delegates, their settings and their locations across England. What was evident was the similarities between SBMs as business leaders (BL) and Head Teachers as business leaders. It also highlighted the evolving skill sets of CEOs of MATs and the requirement for them to understand the SBM competencies to run a MAT. On day 2 I used the analogy of calling them 'Power Rangers', which raised a few eyebrows.

This was broken down into the following:

Power - 'A particular form of energy, capacity to influence.'

Ranger - 'A person who wanders about large areas of country.'

This sums up the role of CEOs and Business Leaders in MATs. The area of *'Power'* is the real catalyst of change and capacity to drive up educational standards within a MAT. The potential of MATs can only be tapped into if there is a shared ethos which runs throughout the whole MAT from top to bottom and there is a real push towards shared services including a central support function. This will mean that in many cases, there will most likely be one business leader supporting the CEO but it is also an opportunity for SBMs to specialise in their areas of expertise. By having one SBL, this will encourage true collaboration and commonality / consistency across a MAT and drive down costs. (Why have eight separate finance teams and eight separate sets of contracts across the MAT when you can have one central team and one set of jointly negotiated contracts?)

If we extend this to the sharing of teaching staff and curriculum specialists, you have a recipe for pure collaboration in improving teaching and learning, delivering effective CPD, increased efficiency of resources, and improving spend across the entire MAT.

The area of *'Ranger'* is where both CEOs and SBLs will spend a lot of their time if they are expanding their MATs, due to the need to scout schools and, believe it or not, initiate a courting process of generating the interest for schools to come into the MAT (a process completely built on trust). This has also become known as 'try before you buy.' Likening the experience to 'Come Dine With Me', the SBLs will be heavily involved in the various due diligences and meetings to be had with counterparts within the incoming schools.

Is organic healthier?

As MATs move away from national expansion to more local and regional expansion, the number of local schools joining local MATs is about to accelerate with finance being one of the main drivers. As finances become more challenging, schools must challenge themselves and ask, what does true collaboration look like? A collaborative model must have system leadership at its core and a desire to collectively procure and share services and specialisms.

As said previously, if you want to see how schools will exist in 15 years' time look at the current NHS model. MAT or no MAT, the legal existence of schools as silos is looking increasingly less likely and more like Hyper Trusts. Finally, what came across strongly from the training was, the most successful MATs grew organically and not too quickly but reflected at every stage of their expansion and constantly reviewed their structures. This definitely sounds like 'morphing time' for the SBL sector.

The CFO stereotype

The CFOs of the past, especially in the private sector, have come from a predominantly financial background with limited operational experience in areas outside of finance. These other areas such as HR, IT and legal, were normally specialisms, which sat within their own respective departments and which had dedicated specialist staff. The SBM is seen as the generalist, but this is where the evolution is beginning to unfold.

The stereotype of the CFO was somebody who would tell you there was not enough budget or produce financial reporting. The CFO of the future within schools must release themselves from this mould in order to express themselves in a way where the organisation can capitalise fully from their skill set. Effective CFOs don't just see themselves as number crunchers, but as strategic players who can bring creative energy and values to a school. There will always be a role for critical routine financial tasks, but the CFO role is more dynamic and broad, covering several important areas of operational strategy.

Today's CFO must be able to take financial information and use it to influence operational decision making as well as strategy. If you take the COO role and add in financial management, you have the CFO role. CFOs are more like business partners to the CEO, who help influence the direction of the organisation.

The CFO competency framework

The following is a list of competencies CFOs will be required to have and develop to be able to carry out the role.

Area of competency	Detail
Governance and Financial assurance	Governance and controls Compliance Audit Policy implementation
Operational leadership	Optimise systems and processes Support functions Lead operations Embed best practice Facilities management Procurement
Organisational leadership	HR Legal Manage people
Strategy and innovation	Data analysis Strategic decision making Critical voice Co-pilot to CEO Maximise value
Business reporting	Financial and non-financial
Technology and risk	Data management and delivery IT Cyber risk management
Behaviours	Soft skills Communication Relationship building

Area of competency	Detail
	Influencer
	Visible leader
	Diplomatic challenger
	Trustworthiness
	Integrity
	Authority
Change driver	Oversee business transformation
	Restructure business operations
	More for less mind-set
	Coach
	Mentor
	Leadership developer
	Finance transformation
	Culture driver
Stakeholder relationship management	Relationship builder and maintainer
	Emotional intelligence
	Know your team
	Self awareness

The CFO – CEO relationship

The role of CFO is continuously evolving, with the remit becoming more variable and strategic. The importance of the CFO role in today's climate is evident when it comes to risk analysis, with this being a standing item at board level. The CFO is able to show the CEO, through a commercial and financial lens, any impacts on the overall business and how future strategy and decision making will need to be shaped in order to protect the business. The CFO is increasingly perceived as a collaborative partner to the CEO, with the relationship being one of the closest and most vital to every element of school business leadership. The individual strengths of the CFO and CEO should complement one another.

Disruptors of the CFO role

As a CFO previously, there are now more things which can disrupt how a business operates which will also impact on the areas of responsibility of the CFO. Data has been at the forefront for the last couple of years with ransomware attacks on schools, and in particular, MATs, increasing exponentially. Such is the concern around this area, it has now been made a reportable item if a ransom demand is made.

The risk and uncertainty in a post-pandemic world will mean more and more areas either coming under attack or at a higher risk than before.

Leading an evolving finance function

Only one in six transactions now take place using cash, and the relationship between IT and finance is changing rapidly. Technological advances have transformed how businesses operate and we have seen a sharp increase in technology usage in 2020. The way this has transformed businesses has gained a lot of momentum and CFOs will be at the heart of both the finance and digital transformations of their organisations.

The relationship between the CFO and the CIO (chief information officer) or IT lead, will be important as organisations seek ways to improve their technology to support more effective and efficient ways of data analysis, communication and decision making.

Abbreviations

ABBLed – Association of BAME Business Leaders in Education

ACS – Average Class Size

ATC – Average Teacher Cost

ATL – Average Teacher Load

BCS – Benchmark Class Size

CB – Curriculum Bonus

CEO – Chief Executive Officer

CFO – Chief Financial Officer

CIO – Chief Information Officer

CIPFA – Chartered Institute of Public Finance and Accountancy

CPD – Continuous Professional Development

CSBM – Certificate in School Business Management

DfE – Department for Education

DSBM – Diploma in School Business Management

ECF – Early Career Framework

EEF – Education Endowment Foundation

ESFA – Education and Skills Funding Agency

FPC – Financial Performance Charter

FSM – Free School Meals

FTE – Full Time Equivalent

GAG – General Annual Grant

HLTA – Higher Level Teaching Assistant

ICFP – Integrated Curriculum Financial Planning

KPI – Key Performance Indicator

LA – Local Authority

LEG – Leadership Efficiency Gearing

MAT – Multi-Academy Trust

NCTL – National College for Teaching and Leadership

NFF – National Funding Formula

NOR – Number on Roll

PAN – Published Admission Number

PP – Pupil Premium

PPA – Planning, Preparation and Assessment

PTR – Pupil Teacher Ratio

RAG – Red, Amber, Green

SAT – Single Academy Trust

SBL – School Business Leader or Leadership

SBM – School Business Manager or Management

SEN – Special Educational Needs

SFVS – Schools Financial Value Standard

TL – Teacher Load

TLR – Teaching and Learning Responsibility Payment

TMS – Teachers Main Scale

TSR – Teacher Support Staff Ratio

Printed in Great Britain
by Amazon

24444870R00076